Map Smart

World Maps

Nicolas Brasch

A⁺

Smart Apple Media
P.O. Box 3263
Mankato, MN, 56002

First published in 2011 by
MACMILLAN EDUCATION AUSTRALIA PTY LTD
15–19 Claremont St, South Yarra, Australia 3141

Visit our web site at www.macmillan.com.au or go directly to www.macmillanlibrary.com.au

Associated companies and representatives throughout the world.

Copyright text © Nicolas Brasch 2011

Library of Congress Cataloging-in-Publication Data
  Brasch, Nicolas.
  World maps / by Nicolas Brasch.
    p. cm. -- (Map smart)
  Includes index.
   Summary: "Gives information on types and features of world maps. Includes quizzes and a mapmaking activity"--Provided by publisher.
  ISBN 978-1-59920-416-1 (library binding)
  1. Cartography--Juvenile literature. 2. World maps--Juvenile literature. I. Title.
   GA105.6.B745 2012
   912--dc22
                        2010049984 .

Publisher: Carmel Heron
Commissioning Editor: Niki Horin
Managing Editor: Vanessa Lanaway
Editor: Laura Jeanne Gobal
Proofreader: Georgina Garner

Designer: Colby Heppell (text and cover)
Page Layout: Romy Pearse
Photo Researcher: Jes Senbergs (management: Debbie Gallagher)
Illustrator: Ian Faulkner (www.ianfaulknerillustrator.com)
Production Controller: Vanessa Johnson

Manufactured in China by Macmillan Production (Asia) Ltd.
Kwun Tong, Kowloon, Hong Kong
Supplier Code: CP December 2010

Acknowledgments

The author and the publisher are grateful to the following for permission to reproduce copyright material:

Front cover photograph: Earth and moon courtesy of Dreamstime.com/Uzuri.

Photographs courtesy of: Getty Images/Blend Images/Sam Bloomberg-Rissman, **4** (left); iStockPhoto/Onur Döngel, **18**, /Uli Hamacher, **24**; NASA, **8**, **10** (left); Photolibrary/Mark and Audrey Gibson, **16**, /Westend61, **4** (right); Shutterstock, **25** (bottom left), /CG-Art, **25** (middle right), /S. Hanusch, **25** (middle bottom left), /Jazzia, **25** (middle left), **25** (middle top left), /Cecilia Lim H. M., **25** (middle centre right), /Markov, **25** (middle bottom right), /Monkey Business Images, **5**, /Stoyanh, **25** (bottom right), /John T. Takai, **25** (middle top right), /Evgeny Vasenev, **4** (middle); USGS, **10** (right), **12**.

While every care has been taken to trace and acknowledge copyright, the publisher tenders their apologies for any accidental infringement where copyright has proved untraceable. They would be pleased to come to a suitable arrangement with the rightful owner in each case.

Please note
At the time of printing, the Internet addresses appearing in this book were correct. Owing to the dynamic nature of the Internet, however, we cannot guarantee that all these addresses will remain correct.

Contents

When a word is printed in **bold**, you can look up its meaning in the Glossary on page 31.

Be "Map Smart"

Are you "map smart?" Knowing about maps and how to read them is very important. There will be many times in our lives when we will need to use a map. Being "map smart" is a useful skill for life.

What Is a Map?

A map is a drawing of something that gives a person a view of it from above. A map can show the shape and location of countries, small areas of land, natural features, such as rivers, and artificial features, such as roads. There are many types of maps for many different uses.

A map can guide people from one place to another. It can show them where different places are and how far away one place is from another. Maps can save people time and energy by helping them not get lost.

Maps are available in many different forms and people use them in different ways.

Hi! My name is Mapolean, but you can call me Map. I'll pop up from time to time to give you some tips on being "map smart."

World Maps

World maps are drawings of the whole world. They show people how the world is divided into **continents** and countries.

What Do World Maps Show?

World maps show people the world's many features. Some of these features are natural. Others are determined by humans. These features may include:

- major cities
- **elevation** and depth
- large bodies of water
- distances between countries, cities, and other places
- national **borders**

TRY THIS

Look at a map of the world. Which country has the most shared borders?

Answer: China and the Russian Federation both share borders with 14 countries. Don't forget there is a part of the Russian Federation located between Poland and Lithuania!

When Do People Use World Maps?

People can use world maps to help them locate continents, countries, and oceans. They also use a world map if they are planning a holiday abroad and they want to choose a country to visit or find out how far away a country is.

It is helpful to know where different places are in the world so that people can understand how an event in one country can affect another country, including their own.

Types of World Maps

There are many types of world maps. Some world maps show people where all the continents, countries, oceans, major seas, and large deserts are. Other world maps show people national borders. Some world maps focus on elevation or the types of **industries** in different parts of the world. Other world maps focus on **climate**.

Climate Maps

Climate maps provide information about rainfall, temperature, and other weather-related features in different parts of the world. They often use color to highlight climate differences.

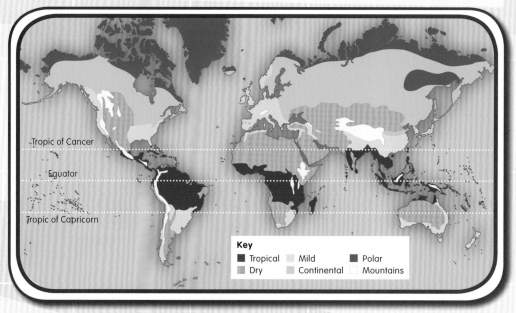

Key

■ Tropical   ■ Mild   ■ Polar
■ Dry   ■ Continental   □ Mountains

This climate map divides the world into six climatic types, each represented by a different color.

The Tropics of Cancer and Capricorn

The Tropic of Cancer is an imaginary line that marks the most northerly point at which the sun can be seen directly overhead. Similarly, the Tropic of Capricorn marks the most southerly point at which the sun can be seen directly overhead.

Natural Resources Maps

Natural resources maps provide information about the natural resources that can be found in different parts of the world. These natural resources include minerals, found in the ground, and oil, which may be found in the ground or beneath the sea. Symbols are usually used to identify where natural resources are found.

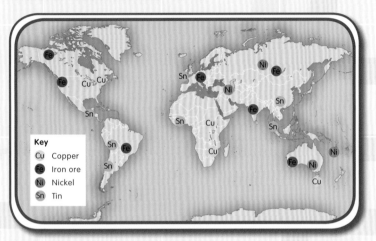

TRY THIS

Transporting natural resources costs a lot of money, so countries try to buy natural resources from areas closest to them. Find a natural resources map of the world and look for your country's nearest oil, coal, and gas supplies. If they are within your country, find the locations closest to you.

This natural resources map shows the types of minerals that can be found in some countries around the world. The minerals are represented by their chemical symbols. The guide to these symbols can be found in the box on the left of the map.

Economic Maps

Economic maps provide information about the types of industries in each country, the amount of money people earn, or some other feature of a country's economy. Symbols or colors are usually used to identify differences in industries or money earned.

This economic map sorts the world according to the amount of money people earn, or their income. People living in areas colored green have the lowest income, while those living in areas colored purple have the highest income.

Physical Maps

Physical maps focus on the types of natural features that exist around the world. These features include mountains, hills, and bodies of water. Colors are usually used to identify different natural features.

Many physical maps focus on **topography**. Topographic maps show how elevation changes in a country.

This topographic map was created using special cameras on board a **satellite** traveling around Earth in space. Low elevations are shown in purple, medium elevations are green and yellow, and high elevations are orange, red, and white.

How many separate images do you think were used to create this topographic map of the world? If you guessed nearly 1.2 million images, you're right!

Political Maps

Political maps use colors and lines to show where national borders begin and end. Some also name every country. Some political maps identify national **capitals**. These capitals are usually marked by a large circle or star. Detailed political maps also include state borders and state capitals.

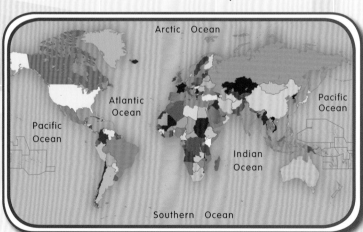

This simple political map of the world shows every country and the oceans. Each country is a different color so that its borders can be clearly seen.

Population Maps

Population maps show how many people live in different countries. Cartographers usually use colors to show changes in population in different countries.

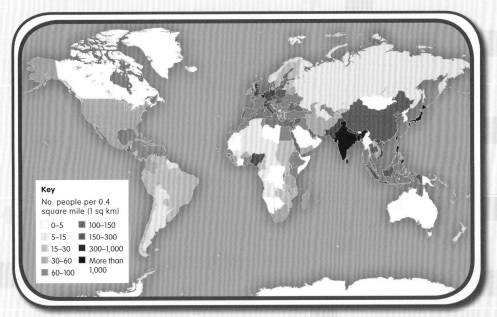

Key
No. people per 0.4 square mile (1 sq km)

- 0–5
- 5–15
- 15–30
- 30–60
- 60–100
- 100–150
- 150–300
- 300–1,000
- More than 1,000

This population map uses color to show areas of high and low population in the world. The white countries are the least populated, with 0 to 5 people per 0.4 square mile (1 sq km). The dark brown countries are the most heavily populated, with more than 1,000 people per 0.4 square mile (1 sq km).

Other World Maps

There are many other types of world maps that provide all sorts of information. There are maps that focus on the religions practiced in different parts of the world, the languages spoken, time zones, and even the rate of home ownership. In fact, there are world maps for almost every topic people can think of!

Did you know that a person who create maps is called a cartographer (*car-tog-ra-fa*)? The word "cartographer" comes from the French word *carte*, meaning "map."

How Is a World Map Created?

There are seven main stages involved in creating a world map. The stages that involve drawing the map are done by a cartographer.

Stage 1: Deciding On the Type of Map

The first thing a cartographer does is decide what type of world map he or she is going to create. Satellites, which take photos of Earth from space, take many types of photos, which the cartographer can use to create maps. To create a physical map, the cartographer needs satellite photos of mountains, hills, bodies of water, and other natural features. To create an economic map, the cartographer needs to find an organization that collects and stores information related to economies.

Since the 1950s, humans have sent satellites into space. Cameras on satellites can take photos of Earth.

Early World Maps

Before the use of satellites, world maps were created by people who traveled around on foot, horseback, in boats, and in airplanes, noting every feature they passed. Their world maps did not include every location on Earth, only those that they knew existed. As new discoveries were made, world maps become more accurate, or correct.

This is an example of a satellite image. It shows a part of Africa (bottom left), the Arabian Peninsula, and a part of Asia (on the right).

Stage 2: Deciding What To Include on the Map

Once the cartographer has decided on the type of map to be created, he or she will have a good idea of what the map should show. However, the cartographer will need to exclude some items from the map because there will not be enough space to show everything. For example, not every city will be included on a political map. Only major cities might be shown.

TRY THIS

Get a map of the world and a map of the country you live in. Compare the two. What features on the country map are not included on the world map?

This world map is very hard to read because it includes the names of too many cities and towns!

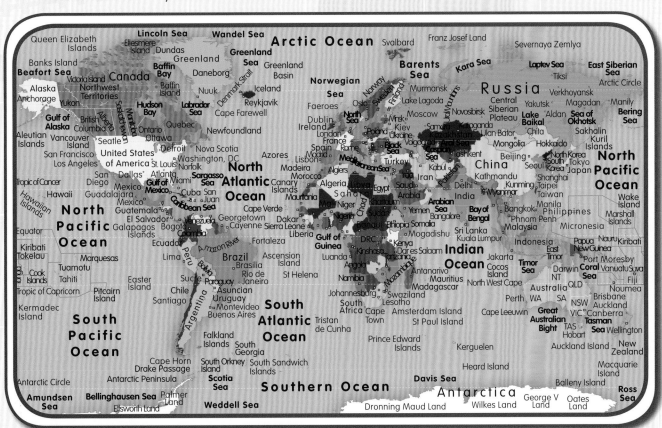

Stage 3: Measuring Distances

On a world map, the length of national borders and the distances between capitals and other features have to be accurate. If these are wrong, the map will not provide readers with a true picture of the world. Cartographers get the right information from satellites and electronic **surveying** equipment, and from companies and government departments that collect and store such information.

Countries with a coastline do not end where the land ends. All of the sea up to 12 **nautical miles** from the coastline belongs to that country. Some maps may have a shaded area that represents these **territorial waters**.

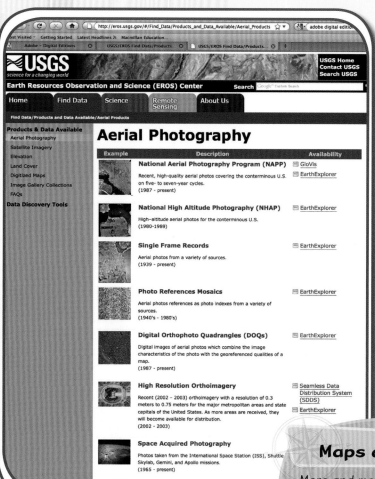

The United States Geological Service (USGS) has all sorts of useful information and images for cartographers preparing maps of the United States.

Maps and the Internet

More and more mapping information is now provided online. Before the Internet, new information had to be included in the next edition of printed maps. This could take months or even years to reach the public. Now, people can get this new information much more quickly.

Stage 4: Deciding On the Scale of the Map

The **scale** of a map is the relationship between the sizes of the features on the map and their sizes in **reality**. The features cannot be drawn to their actual sizes, so the cartographer has to shrink them. Every feature must be shrunk by exactly the same amount to make the map as accurate as possible.

The scale is usually represented on the map in figures. If the scale on a map is 1:1,000,000, it means the features on the map are 1,000,000 times smaller than they are in reality.

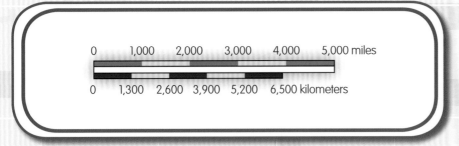

Sometimes the scale takes the form of a bar that shows what distance each centimeter or inch on the map represents. This scale shows that 1 inch is equal to 2,000 miles.

Get someone to measure your height and then measure his or her height. Draw a picture of the two of you to scale. If your height in the picture is going to be one-tenth of your real height, then it has to be reduced by 90 percent. For example, if you are 54 inches (137 cm) tall, your height in the picture should be 5.4 inches (13.7 cm).

Try This

Stage 5: Choosing Symbols for the Map

Symbols are pictures or patterns on a map that represent particular features. Cartographers have to decide what these symbols should be.

Symbols have to be easy to understand and are usually linked to the feature they represent. For example, on a world map, airports might be represented by a picture of an airplane.

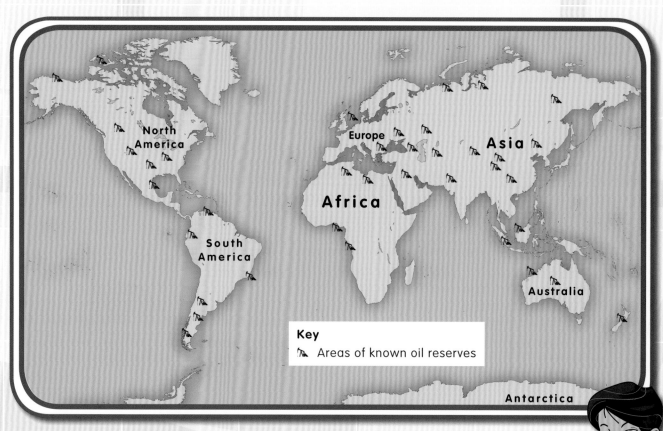

North America

Europe

Asia

Africa

South America

Australia

Key

⚒ Areas of known oil reserves

Antarctica

This map shows where oil is found in the world. The symbol used to represent the locations is an oil well.

TRY THIS

Symbols do not just appear on maps. They are all around us on street signs, posters, and even electronic equipment. Can you find examples of symbols in your daily life?

Stage 6: Checking the Accuracy of the Map

Once the map is ready, it is checked to make sure there are no mistakes. For example, on a natural resources map, the cartographer should check that the locations of mineral deposits have been plotted accurately. The cartographer should also check that:

- the names of countries, cities, major towns, mountains, oceans, and other features are spelled correctly and that these features are in the right places
- national borders are in the right places
- the lengths of the borders are accurate
- the distances between cities are accurate
- symbols are placed in the right positions

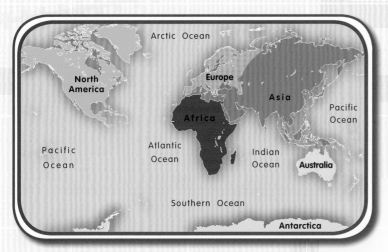

Can you spot the mistake on this map of the world's continents? It is missing South America! If this map were printed with such a mistake, the people of South America would be very upset.

Correcting the mistake on this map would be very costly if it had already been printed and released!

Stage 7: Updating the Map

Keeping maps up-to-date is very important. Minerals are found in new locations every year, so natural resources maps need to be updated. The names of major cities might change, so political maps need to be updated. After wars, maps often have to be redrawn because of changes to national borders.

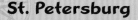

St. Petersburg

The city of St. Petersburg in the Russian Federation has changed its name several times after changes of government. Over the last 100 years, it has been called St. Petersburg (before 1914 and since 1991), Petrograd (1914–24) and Leningrad (1924–91).

Features of World Maps

World maps have many features to help people read and understand them. Cartographers decide which features to use depending on the types of maps they are creating.

Using Shortcuts

Cartographers use simple designs to represent different map features. Once people know what the designs represent, they can look at a map and immediately understand it. They can think of map features as shortcuts. The main features of most world maps are:

- a compass rose
- a grid
- longitude and latitude
- a scale
- elevation and depth
- different colors

A cartographer works with some very basic features to represent information on a map.

An Inset

When there is too much information about a country to fit on a map, the information may be placed in a box outside the map. This box is called an inset. For example, the state of Hawaii may not fit on a map of the United States and may be placed in an inset.

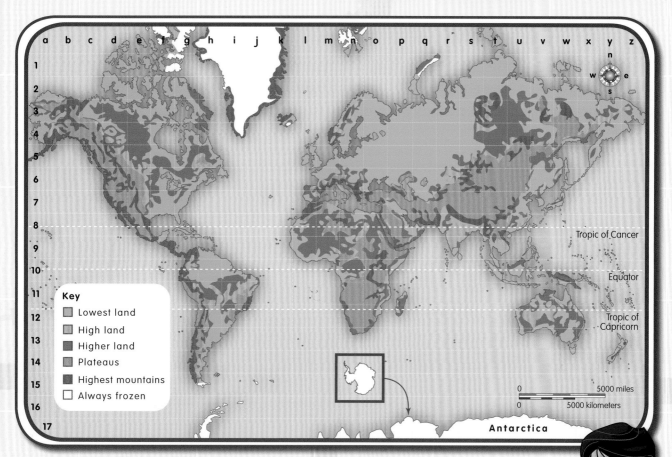

Map labels:

a b c d e f g h i j k l m n o p q r s t u v w x y z

1 2 3 4 5 6 7 8 9 10 11 12 13 14 15 16 17

n
w e
s

Tropic of Cancer

Equator

Tropic of Capricorn

Key
☐ Lowest land
☐ High land
☐ Higher land
☐ Plateaus
☐ Highest mountains
☐ Always frozen

0   5000 miles
0   5000 kilometers

Antarctica

This map of the world shows elevation through the use of colors. It also shows the **equator** and tropics of Cancer and Capricorn, which are latitude lines. The map also contains a compass rose, grid, key, scale, and inset.

Find a world political map with every country and major city named. Then take an "A" to "Z" trip around the world, beginning at a country or city that starts with "A," then moving on to "B," and all the way to "Z!"

TRY THIS

Another feature that maps have is a key, which is also known as a legend. The key explains what each of the symbols on a map means.

Compass Rose

A compass rose is a feature on a map that indicates direction, such as north, south, west, and east. It shows readers the direction they have to follow to get from one place to another. A compass rose may be placed in a corner of a world map.

The directions on a compass rose are based on those found on a compass. A compass is a device that tells people which way is north, no matter where they are.

There are usually eight points on a compass: N (north), S (south), W (west), E (east), NW (northwest), NE (northeast), SW (southwest), and SE (southeast).

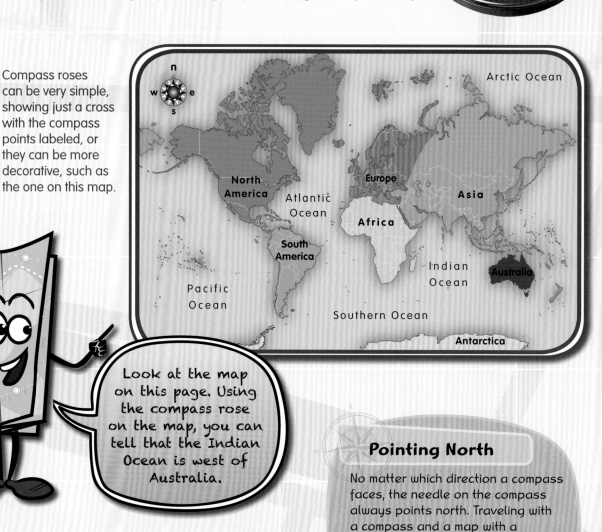

Compass roses can be very simple, showing just a cross with the compass points labeled, or they can be more decorative, such as the one on this map.

Look at the map on this page. Using the compass rose on the map, you can tell that the Indian Ocean is west of Australia.

Pointing North

No matter which direction a compass faces, the needle on the compass always points north. Traveling with a compass and a map with a compass rose will help people reach their destination!

Grid

A grid is a pattern of **horizontal** and **vertical** lines that forms a series of squares, columns and rows. Each column is given a letter, starting from "A." Each row is given a number, starting from "1."

Locations on a map are often given a grid reference. For example, if a country is in section F6 on a map, the reader should find the square where column F and row 6 meet. The country will be within that square.

TRY THIS

Using the map below, list the grid references for Colombia, Malaysia, and Norway.

Answers:
Colombia—D5;
Sri Lanka—I5;
Poland—G2.

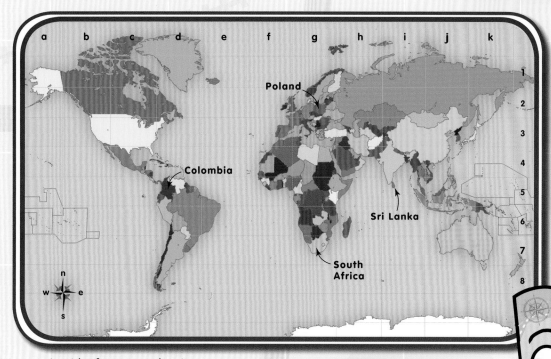

A grid reference makes it easy to find something on a map.

On this map, South Africa is in section G7. To find South Africa on this map, move one finger down column G and another finger along row 7. The point where your fingers meet forms section G7. South Africa is in this section.

Latitude and Longitude

Latitude and longitude are imaginary lines that run across Earth. They help people to locate places.

Latitude lines are **horizontal** lines. They show how far north or south a place is from the **equator**. Longitude lines are **vertical** lines. They show how far east or west a place is from Greenwich, England. The farther away a place is from the equator or Greenwich, the higher its latitude or longitude numbers will be.

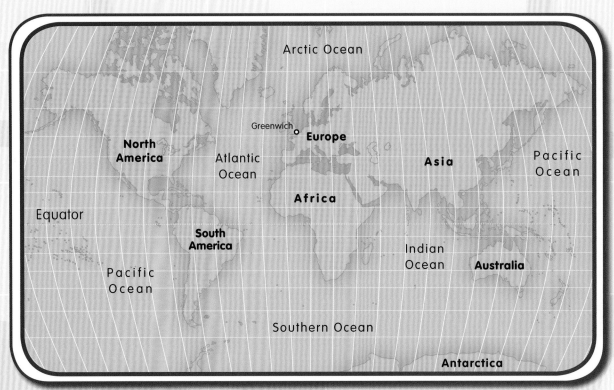

In 1884, Greenwich was chosen as the point at which longitude lines start. It was chosen because it was home to a huge observatory with very accurate measuring equipment.

Degrees and Minutes

Latitude and longitude are expressed in degrees and minutes. These do not have anything to do with temperature or time. Instead, they relate to distance. Degrees are indicated by the symbol ° and minutes are indicated by the symbol '. For example, the latitude and longitude for Berlin, Germany, are latitude 52°30'N; longitude 13°25'E. "N" stands for north and "E" stands for east.

Scale

The scale of a map is the amount by which it is smaller than the area it represents. It is important that everything on a map is reduced by the same amount. If two countries were reduced by different amounts, one country may look larger than the other one on a map even though it may be smaller in **reality**. Reducing everything by the same amount also ensures that the distances between the features on a map are accurate.

The scale of a map is usually represented by a bar scale that shows how much each inch or centimeter on a map represents in reality.

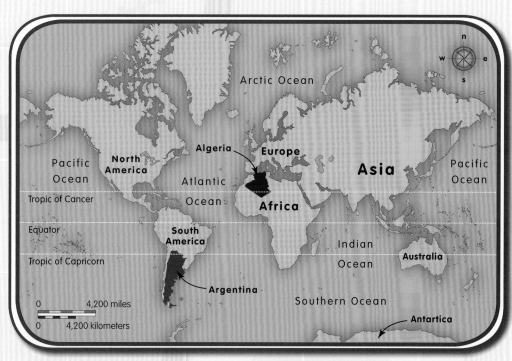

On this map of the world, the scale is 0.43 inches (1.1 cm) to 2,796 miles (4,200 km). This means 0.43 inches on the map is equal to 2,796 miles (4,200 km) in reality.

Using a ruler and the scale on this map, figure out the distance between Algeria and Argentina. Is your answer about 6,000 miles (10,000 km)? If it is, you're right!

Elevation and Depth

Although a map is flat, the area that it represents is usually not flat. On a topographic world map, there are many mountains of different heights. The elevation of these mountains has to be shown on the map. Oceans have varying depths. They are much shallower close to land. Depth is also shown on a topographic map.

On world maps, elevation and depth are usually represented in different shades of colors. Sometimes depth is indicated by numbers representing the depth in feet or meters.

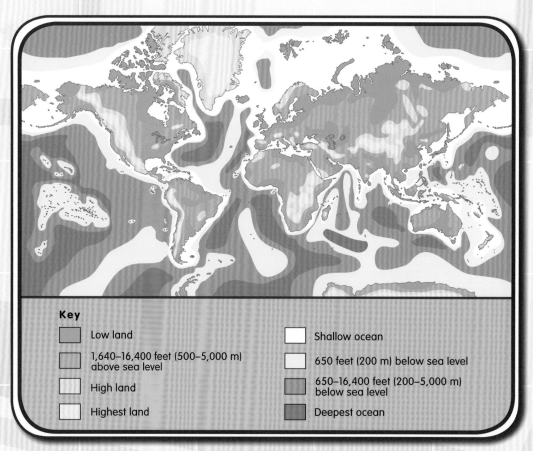

Key

Low land	Shallow ocean
1,640–16,400 feet (500–5,000 m) above sea level	650 feet (200 m) below sea level
High land	650–16,400 feet (200–5,000 m) below sea level
Highest land	Deepest ocean

On this map, the key tells us what the colors on the map represent. Changes in elevation are shown using green, brown, pink, and pale brown, and changes in depth are shown using white, blue, and purple.

Colors

Colors are used on maps to help identify different features quickly and easily. For example, on a political map, one country may be colored pink, while a neighboring country may be colored green. This makes it easy for readers to see where the national borders are.

Color is also used to make sure there is a clear difference between similar features. For example, rivers and highways may be drawn in two different colors so they cannot be mixed up. If they were the same color, it would be hard to tell which was which.

The British Empire

During the late 1800s and early 1900s, many maps of the world had large areas of land colored pink. These lands were the **colonies** of the British Empire. Visit http://en.wikipedia.org/wiki/File:The_British_Empire.png to see these pink areas.

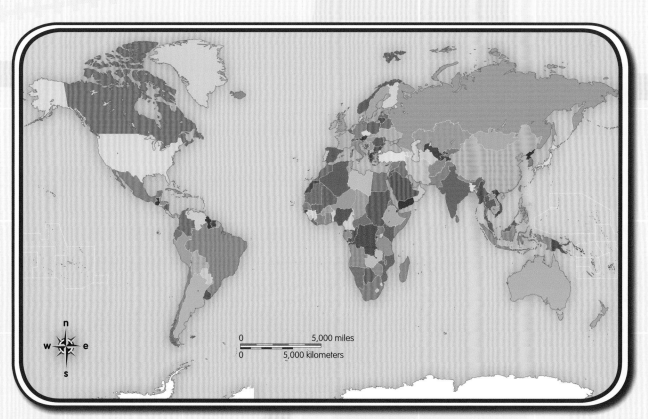

The use of color on this political map makes it easy to tell one country from another.

Symbols on World Maps

Symbols are pictures or patterns that represent particular features. They are used to help readers understand a map.

Quick and Easy

Symbols save cartographers time. For example, by using an airplane to represent an airport, a cartographer does not have to spend time surveying the airport to draw it accurately on a map. Symbols need to be simple and easily recognized by readers.

Symbols are not just found on maps. There are symbols around people every day, such as on street signs. How many symbols can you spot on your way to and from school?

What Is a Globe?

A globe is a world map printed on an object shaped like a ball. It is more accurate than a flat map because a globe has the same shape as Earth.

Symbols help people to understand a map written in their own language and they help people to understand maps written in other languages too. People may not always understand words, but many symbols represent the same things around the world!

Guess the Symbols

Here are some symbols that you might find on a world map. Can you guess what they represent? There is a clue with each one.

(a) This type of road carries more vehicles further and faster than other roads.

(b) "Toot, toot!"

(c) The natural resource obtained from this location can be used to make electricity.

(d) These natural movements of water push ships and other vessels in certain directions.

(e) A large ship can enter one of these.

(f) These lines officially separate countries.

(g) This is where people try to "slide" off a mountain!

(h) You will need a lot of energy to get to the top of this.

(i) A shiny, precious jewel is found in the ground here.

(j) Stand by for a bumpy landing!

(k) A place where animals can be found in their natural habitat.

(l) Most vehicles need what comes out of this structure to get going.

Check your answers!
(a) a highway *(b)* a railway track *(c)* a coal-mining area *(d)* ocean currents *(e)* a harbor or port
(f) national borders *(g)* a ski area *(h)* a mountain *(i)* a diamond mine *(j)* an airport *(k)* a wildlife reserve
(l) an oil well

Reading World Maps

Now that you have learned about the different parts of a map, it is time to try reading a world map.

Finding Your Way

World maps may have a number of common features:

- The compass rose indicates which way north, south, west, and east lie.

- Countries can be told apart through the use of color.

- The horizontal lines are the lines of latitude. The vertical lines are the lines of longitude.

- The bar at the bottom shows the scale of the map.

0   5,000 miles

0   5,000 kilometers

Look at the map on page 27. What is the least number of countries you would have to cross to get from Tanzania to Nigeria (including Tanzania and Nigeria)?

Go to http://www.theodora.com/maps/new5/802649.jpg Can you guess what this map of the world shows?

Answer: It is a map of the world's 24 time zones, with each zone representing one hour of difference.

TRY THIS

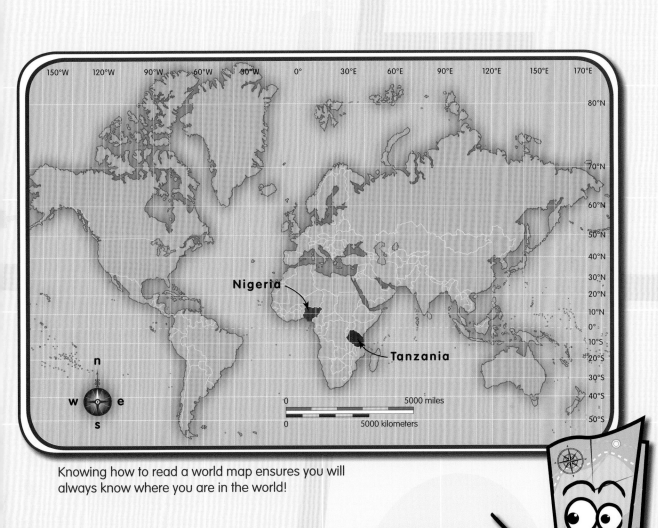

Knowing how to read a world map ensures you will always know where you are in the world!

You would have to cross six countries to get from Tanzania to Nigeria!

ACTIVITY: Create a World Map

Now that you know how world maps are created, it is your turn to be a cartographer. Your challenge is to create an imaginary world!

Materials You Will Need:
- large sheet of paper
- pen or pencil
- calculator
- colored pens or pencils
- ruler
- your imagination!

STEP 1

Draw an Imaginary World

Draw an imaginary world on the large sheet of paper. It can have as many continents, countries, and oceans as you like. Color your countries.

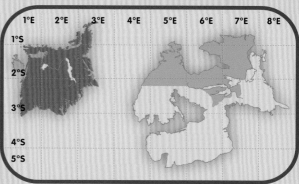

STEP 2

Add Lines

Draw the latitude and longitude lines on your world map. At the end of each line, write the number of degrees that the line represents. Make the difference between each line one degree. These lines can also be the grid.

Step 3 · Decide On the Scale of Your Map

Decide how long or wide your world should be. Next, measure the width of the world you have drawn on your map. Let's say you decide your world is 400 miles (645 km) wide in reality and on your map it is 4 inches (10 cm) wide. This means 1 inch is equal to 100 miles (161 km) or 1 cm is equal to 40 miles (64.4 km). Draw the scale in a corner of your map.

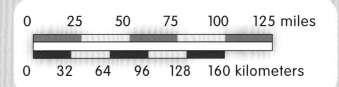

Step 4 · Add Symbols

Decide on the symbols you wish to use. How would you like to represent oceans, mountains, national borders, and capitals? Are you going to include symbols showing economic activity?

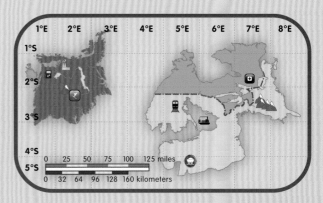

Step 5 · Add Some Fun Names

Name the continents, countries, cities, some mountains, and even some bodies of water in your world. Your world map is now ready for use! Where will your imagination take you next?

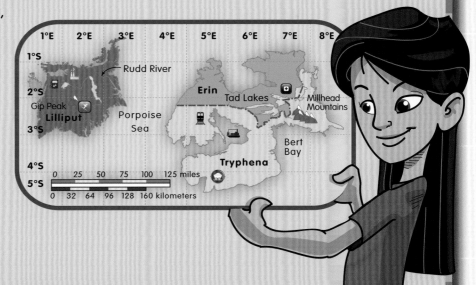

Quiz: Are You "Map Smart?"

Try this quiz and test your knowledge of world maps! All of the answers can be found in this book. Write your answers on a piece of paper and turn to page 32 to check if you are right. If you answer all 10 questions correctly, you can consider yourself "map smart!"

1 What do the letters NW stand for?

2 What is another word for height?

3 Does the grid square Q4 appear closer to the right or left of a map?

4 True or false? The vertical and horizontal lines on a map are known as tudelongi and tudelati?

5 If cartographers have too much information, where can they fit some of the extra information?

6 Is a scale included on a map to show that things on the map are bigger or smaller than they are in reality?

7 Which color commonly represents oceans on a world map?

8 What does this symbol stand for on a world map?

9 What type of map shows how many people live in each country?

10 What does this symbol stand for on a map?

Good-bye! This is where I leave you. I am sure you are now "map smart." The next time someone asks you for directions or asks you to draw a community map, you should know exactly what to do. Well done!

Glossary

borders
imaginary lines that separate countries and states

capitals
cities or towns that are the official seat of government of a country or state

climate
the normal weather conditions in a particular area

colonies
countries or areas controlled by another country

continents
large landmasses on Earth, such as Africa, Antarctica, Asia, Australia, Europe, North America, and South America, which are usually surrounded by sea and contain various countries

economic
to do with trade, industry, and making and spending money

elevation
height above sea level

equator
an imaginary line drawn around Earth, midway between the North and South poles

horizontal
flat or level, parallel to the ground

industries
large business activities focused on a particular type of trade or production

natural resources
the naturally occurring useful wealth of a country or area, such as land, forests, water, and minerals

nautical miles
units of distance used at sea; 1 nautical mile is equal to 6,080 feet (1,852 m)

political
to do with the way a country is governed, or ruled

population
all of the people living in a particular country or area

reality
real life

satellite
an artificial object sent into space that travels around Earth and usually collects information

scale
the relationship between the size of something on a map and its size in reality

surveying
measuring the features of an area of land to accurately determine the distances and angles between them

territorial waters
areas of oceans or seas belonging to a particular country

topography
the appearance of natural features on an area of land, particularly the shape of the land's surface

vertical
pointing straight up and down

Index

Answers to the quiz on page 30: 1. northwest 2. elevation 3. right 4. False: They are known as longitude and latitude. 5. in insets 6. smaller 7. blue 8. an area that has a harbor or port deep enough to take large ships 9. population 10. an area known for its coal-mining industry